Published in the United States by Clarkson N. Potter, Inc., 225 Park Avenue South,
New York, New York 10003, and represented in Canada by the Canadian MANDA Group

Published in Great Britain by MacDonald and Co (Publishers) Ltd as
Bellamy's Changing World: The Forest

CLARKSON N. POTTER, POTTER, and colophon are trademarks of Clarkson N. Potter, Inc.

Conceived, edited, and produced by Frances Lincoln Limited,
Apollo Works, 5 Charlton Kings Road,
London NW5, England.

Manufactured in Italy

Library of Congress Cataloging-in-Publication Data

Bellamy, David J.
   The forest.
   (Our changing world)
   Summary: Describes the co-existence of a variety of
plants and animals in their natural forest environment
and their struggle to survive a man-made catastrophe.
   1. Forest ecology – Juvenile literature. 2. Man –
Influence on nature – Juvenile literature. [1. Forest
ecology. 2. Man – Influence on nature. 3. Ecology]
I. Dow, Jill, ill. II. Title. III. Series: Bellamy,
David J. Our changing world.
QH541.5.F6B45 1988   574.5'2642   87-21835
ISBN 0-517-56800-4

10 9 8 7 6 5 4 3 2 1

First Edition

OUR
CHANGING
WORLD

The
FOREST

by DAVID BELLAMY

with illustrations by Jill Dow

Clarkson N. Potter, Inc./Publishers
DISTRIBUTED BY CROWN PUBLISHERS, INC., NEW YORK

It's a fine spring day and the forest is home to many animals and birds. In some areas, foresters are working: cutting trees and planting new ones to provide paper, timber, and firewood for the world outside. Here, some visitors have found a beautiful place for a picnic under a huge oak tree.

The oak is very old and is like a world in itself. High on its branches, the rooks feed their babies. A woodpecker drills into a dead branch to find grubs to eat, and a squirrel, who was busy eating the leaf buds, chases away a great tit. Even the yellow fungus is feeding on the dead wood.

Every year the old tree grows new bark, wood, and leaves. These provide food for many different insects like shield bugs, caterpillars, and leaf miners. It's a good thing that the birds like to eat these insects or there would be far too many and they could kill the trees.

Roller caterpillars hide from the birds by wrapping themselves up in the leaves while they turn into moths. Some insects lay their eggs in the softer parts of the buds, leaves, and twigs. The tree then grows a lump or gall around the eggs, which protects them till they hatch. Leafy trees like the oak are the only place in which many of these creatures can make their home.

1 shield bug   2 leaf miner   3 oak bush cricket   4 roller caterpillar
5 hairstreak caterpillar   6 oak flowers   7 gall wasp
8 oak apple gall   9 marble gall   10 spangle gall

More small creatures live among the mosses and lichens on the oak tree's trunk. Millions of tiny green plants cover the side of the trunk where the rainwater runs down, and the tree creeper climbs up hunting for insects. On the other side, the lace-web spider sits by her trap waiting for something to drop in, and the long-legged harvestmen hunt among the moss. The peppered moth is nearly invisible against the bark.

The bark protects the trunk and branches and makes a firm foothold for all the mosses and lichens, while ferns and other plants root in the cracks. As the tree grows taller and broader, the old bark splits and new layers grow to fill the cracks.

High up, the wood pigeon is sitting on her eggs. She knows that squirrels like to eat eggs and even baby birds.

It's nearly midsummer and the oak has grown many juicy new leaves. The old leaves have been eaten by so many insects that they are in tatters. The cushions of moss clinging to the bark have grown capsules on delicate stalks. When the capsules are ripe they open, releasing thousands of spores which blow onto other twigs and new bare bark, where they grow into new moss plants.

Under the trees it is cool and shady, even in midsummer. A young deer comes to graze on the fresh green grass. Most of the plants already bear fruits and seeds. They flowered in spring before the leaves shut out the sunlight.

Last year's fallen leaves have almost disappeared. Pulled underground and eaten by earthworms, the leaves enrich the soil. The acorns have gone, too, all except one which has taken root beneath its parent oak tree. At first the seedling fed on the fat acorn. Now, its new leaves make their own food from the dappled sunlight that filters down. The young tree grows very slowly, but one day, if it survives, it could take the place of one of the giant old forest oaks, blown down by a storm. Not all acorns grow up into trees: if they did there would soon be no room in the forest.

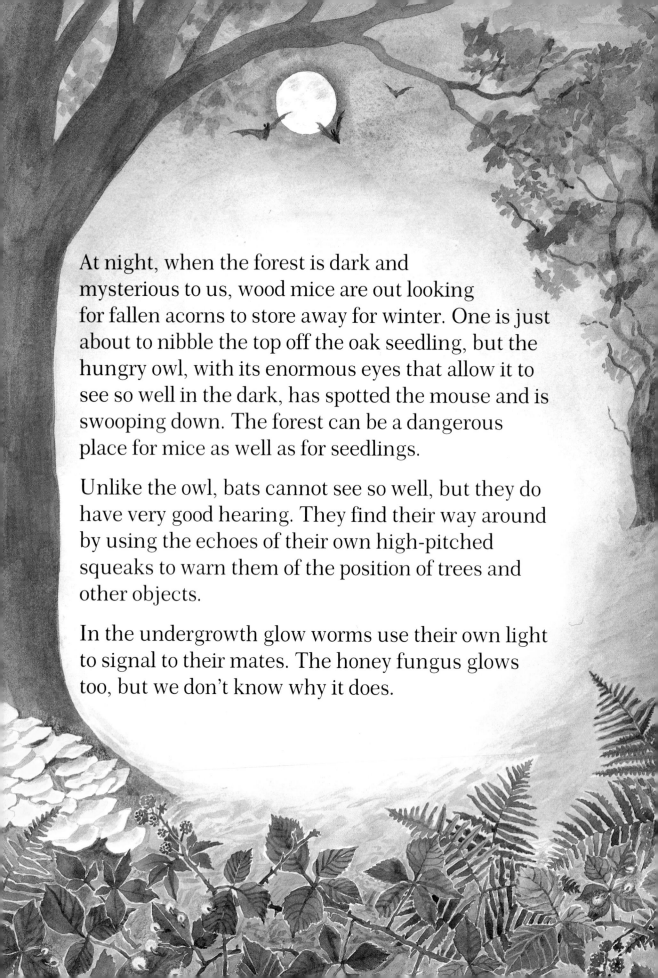

At night, when the forest is dark and
mysterious to us, wood mice are out looking
for fallen acorns to store away for winter. One is just
about to nibble the top off the oak seedling, but the
hungry owl, with its enormous eyes that allow it to
see so well in the dark, has spotted the mouse and is
swooping down. The forest can be a dangerous
place for mice as well as for seedlings.

Unlike the owl, bats cannot see so well, but they do
have very good hearing. They find their way around
by using the echoes of their own high-pitched
squeaks to warn them of the position of trees and
other objects.

In the undergrowth glow worms use their own light
to signal to their mates. The honey fungus glows
too, but we don't know why it does.

In autumn there is plenty of food around, but winter is not far away. The fallen leaves are white with last night's frost. The toads have found a safe place under the leaves to spend the winter and the mice have stocked their burrows with food and grass for nests. The squirrels are collecting acorns and toadstools: they know which toadstools are safe to eat.

We can see only the umbrella or bracket of the toadstool —
that's the part that sticks up into the air. But underneath the
fallen leaves, tiny rootlike threads spread out and feed on
dead material. Toadstools help to keep the forest neat and
the soil fertile. Without them the trees would soon be buried
in dead leaves, twigs, and branches.

On a sunny day in late winter the forest stirs in
its winter sleep. The bats hang silently in the hollow
tree trunk and the squirrels are hidden in their untidy
nest of leaves and twigs, but a winter moth is out enjoying
the sunshine. A tortoiseshell butterfly has been tempted out
by the sun. But will it be able to find the flowers it needs to
feed on? People are busy in the forest, too, and the foresters'
saws can be heard in the distance.

A fieldfare and a blackbird have come to eat the ripe black
fruit of the ivy. Higher up, a mistle thrush pecks at the
berries of the mistletoe which roots deep into the tree's wood
to draw its sap. Nearby, deer graze around hazel trees which
are already covered with catkins sending clouds of yellow
pollen onto the wind. The oak tree itself will not flower until
spring, though the fat buds promise a good crop of leaves
and acorns.

But the giant oak and its companions will never see another spring or autumn. They have been cut down and sold for timber, and now new trees are being planted in their place. These new trees are conifers. The landowners like them because they grow much faster than the broad-leaved trees and produce their harvest of wood more quickly. But what about all the plants and creatures that lived in and around the oak?

All that's left is a stump showing 202 growth rings — one ring for each year of the oak's life — and a pile of logs. The ground is churned up, and most of the wildlife has fled. Only a few damp-loving plants, like rushes, are thriving, and the jackdaws are busy collecting twigs for their nests nearby.

In time, some creatures, like deer, come into the new plantation to feed on the grass, bilberries, and ferns growing between the young trees. But as the trees get bigger, few plants are able to grow under their dense shade. The needles, when they fall, are so tough that they rot very slowly; the worms avoid them and the soil becomes poorer. The jackdaws and the squirrels —including some red squirrels — soon settle in, but many of the other creatures will have moved to other parts of the forest, or will have died.

With few birds to eat them, pine shoot beetles burrow freely into the tender new twigs, and looper caterpillars and aphids attack the young needles. The young trees are in danger from these harmful pests, although the ladybugs do their best to help by eating the aphids. The foresters use a helicopter to spray the plantation with chemicals to kill the insects — unfortunately they kill ladybugs too.

This part of the plantation is older.
The tall straight spruce trees will make
a fine crop of timber and they provide
a home to some beautiful animals and birds.

The colorful crossbills use their
specially shaped beaks to prise
the seeds out of the cones, while the
crested titmice feed their young in a hole in the
tree. They have to watch out for the goshawk
hunting between the trees and for the sleek pine
marten which will eat almost anything it can catch.
Below them, a pine hawk-moth rests on the trunk,
and under the trees, where little grows, the wood
ants use the dead needles to pile up into nests.

The foresters have fixed bat boxes to the trees for
the bats to live in. They have also built a tall
observation tower, from which they can watch over
the plantation and keep an eye open for trouble,
especially fire.

The view from the tower is breathtaking. The forest ranger is up here. He points out the purple emperor butterflies and the squirrels up in the tops of the trees.

Plantations of spruce, larch, and pine dot the countryside but willow, oak, and alder have been allowed to grow along

the river, providing a home for many of the plants, insects, and animals that would once have lived around the old oak. A grassy clearing around its stump is now used as a picnic site. People come here to set out on the new nature trail and to enjoy everything that the different kinds of forests have to offer.

DISCARD

the o.

the observation towe